THE WOMEN WHO CAUGHT THE BABIES

A STORY OF AFRICAN AMERICAN MIDWIVES

Written by **ELOISE GREENFIELD**   *Artwork by* **DANIEL MINTER**

Alazar®
PRESS

CARRBORO, NORTH CAROLINA

DEDICATIONS

To the ancestors, with love and gratitude.
Eloise Greenfield

To the late Mrs. Ethel and the late Mrs. Vera Swan
who had the skill to catch me as I came
into this world feet first.
Daniel Minter

Printed in Canada

Book design and production by Richard Hendel

Text edited by Jacqueline K. Ogburn

Library of Congress Control Number 2018961301

ISBN 978-0-9977720-7-4

First Edition, 2019

is an imprint of Royal Swan Enterprises, Inc.

201 Orchard Lane, Carrboro, NC 27510

Visit us at www.alazar-press.com

INTRODUCTION

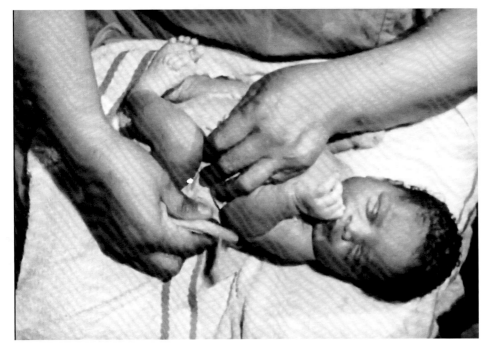

Midwives have been in the world probably as long as there have been human babies on earth. With this book, though, I want to take you back only as far as the Africa of a few hundred years ago. That's when millions of Africans were forced from their homelands, brought to America and enslaved. Some of the enslaved were midwives.

What are midwives? They are women (and some men) who help to bring babies into the world. Midwives use the word "catch" to describe what they do. They say they "catch" the babies, as they are being born.

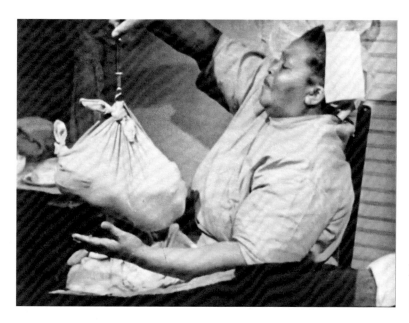

What else do midwives do? Some of their most important duties are to be sure that everything that will touch the baby is free of germs, to encourage the mothers and give them advice, to be watchful and notice if something is going wrong, to place newly born babies on their mothers' chests, to clean the babies,

dress them, wrap them in lightweight blankets, and write down the names the parents give them, the baby's weight, the date and exact time of birth.

During slavery, African American midwives were often women who were no longer young enough to work in the fields. They were called "grannies" and addressed as, "Granny." The name stuck for many years after the end of slavery, even for midwives who were not old enough to be grandmothers. Today, this name is considered by some to be disrespectful, and African American midwives are addressed as "Mrs." or "Miss," followed by their first or last names.

Not all midwives have had the same amount of education. There is a range, from those who have not attended college but learned from other midwives or from public health nurses or doctors to those who have had six or more years of college.

In 1941, the first midwifery training program in the United States, for black public health nurses, was opened in Alabama, at Tuskegee Institute (now Tuskegee University). This institute was founded by famous African American educator, Booker T. Washington.

In earlier centuries, most babies were born with the help of midwives. This continues to be true in many parts of the world, including some countries in Europe. In the United States, however, the great majority of babies are now born in hospitals, with doctors attending. Even so, the number of mothers who prefer to have their babies born at home, or at a birthing center or hospital, with midwives in attendance, is substantial.

Midwives of the past believed that they had been called by God to do their work. Today's midwives may or may not have this belief, but they do consider their work not just a job, but a way of helping others. They are dedicated to the families they serve. The families, in turn, never forget the person who shared with them this time of deep emotion and joy.

Eloise Greenfield

POEMS

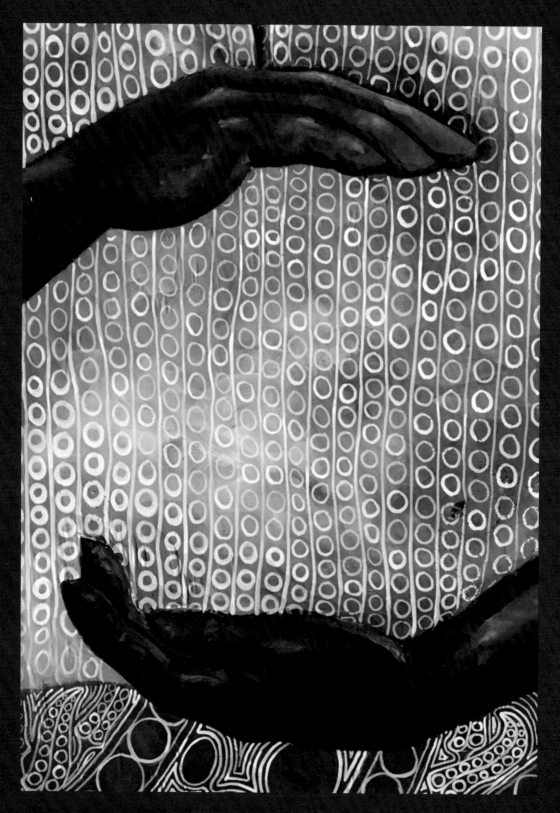

THE WOMEN

They caught the babies,
and catch them still,
welcome them into the world,
for loving.

AFRICA TO AMERICA

Somewhere in the African past,
before the guns, before the
shackles,
before the kidnappings
of story-tellers and sky-readers,
musicians, dancers, doctors,
sculptors, teachers, planters,
hunters, historians,
mothers, fathers and children,
before all that,
there were the women
who caught the babies
and guided them into the world,
with gentle, loving hands.

The women, also kidnapped,
also shackled,
made the torturous voyages
across the ocean into slavery.
In America, African girls
on the brink of womanhood,
watched the women and learned,
then took their turns
at catching the babies,
and so, too, the next generation,
and the next, and the next,
and the next.

AFTER EMANCIPATION, 1863

She, the midwife, felt the
excitement circling through
the room.
She knew the reason,
knew that it was more than
the joy of a new baby coming,
but didn't let herself
think about it yet. She had work
to do.
The mother and the other
women ignored it, too,
until they were sure that
all was well with mother
and baby.
Then they could think,
think about this new thing
that was circling around them.

The grandmother called

the men and children

into the room. The father spoke.

"Our first child born

into freedom," he said.

He knelt and prayed,

the others repeating

after him.

"Thank you, Lord Jesus.

Thank you for this new day,

so long in coming, this

freedom for all of us,

and especially for our

children. Amen. Amen."

THE EARLY 1900s

She waited, not allowing herself
to sleep too deeply.
She knew it was almost time,
that someone would come for her,
if not tonight, then one day
or one night very soon.
She would have to leave quickly.
The baby would not wait.
She had already packed her things,
her stethoscope, her scales
for weighing the baby, and
everything she would need.

She lay there, listening
for the sound of horses' hooves,
or the neighing, and the
banging on the door.
When the sounds came, it was
almost daylight, and when
she climbed into the buggy,
the sky was light enough
for her to see the trees
at the end of the road.

The husband drove the horses
at a medium fast pace,
and got the woman to the house
in time for her to listen
to the beating of the unborn baby's
heart. She examined the mother,
encouraged her to walk around
until it was time for the baby.
When the baby came, the woman
caught him, and guided him
into the world with love.
She laid him on his mother's
chest,
and watched her smile
at this miracle. Her baby.

THE EARLY 2000S

Her cell phone rings. "Hurry!"
the caller says, when the woman
answers. She turns off
the toaster oven. No time now
for dinner. Heavy coat, hat, gloves,
boots. She grabs her bag.
In her car, she eats a cookie,
then two more, hoping she won't
get too hungry, hoping the baby
will come soon, but not too soon.
Not before she gets there.
Mounds of snow and patches
of ice,
still on the ground, from two days
before,
slow the traffic, and she worries
until she is almost there.

The husband's sister greets her
at the door. The woman listens to
the baby's heartbeat, and examines
the mother. Now, the baby
has changed its mind and makes
them wait.
The woman declines an offer
of food. She has forgotten
her hunger.
They wait. One hour. Two. Then,
the woman catches the baby girl,
guides her into the world
with gentle hands and love.
At home, too tired to eat, the woman
showers and goes to bed.
She laughs softly, thinking about
the baby's first cry, a squall,
letting the world know that she is
here. The laughter trails off
into silence,
and the woman sleeps.

THE WOMEN

They caught the babies,
and catch them still,
welcome them into the world,
for loving.

MISS ROVENIA MAYO

If you had asked anybody
in or near the little town
of Parmele, North Carolina,
"Who catches the babies
around here?" they'd
have said, right away,
"Miss Rovenia Mayo. She lives
over yonder." And they'd have
pointed across the fields,
in the direction of her house.
On the evening of May 17, 1929,
Miss Rovenia Mayo caught me,
Eloise.

My great-aunt Mary was there,
and both of my grandmothers.
When my father came home,
later that day, he was glad
to see me, and happy that
Miss Rovenia Mayo
had been there to take care
of Mama and me.

Wilbur Little and Eloise Little, 1929

Weston and Lessie Little with son, Gerald, at Harper's Ferry, 1932

PHOTOGRAPHS

With one exception, the photographs in the introduction were digitally captured from the film All my babies . . . a midwife's own story by documentary filmmaker George C. Stoney. The complete video can be viewed at the Library of Congress website using https://www.loc.gov/item/2017604960/. The photograph of Tuskegee Institute faculty and guests on page 6 is courtesy of Wikimedia Commons.

BIBLIOGRAPHY

BOOKS

Fraser, Gertrude Jacinta. *African American Midwifery in the South: Dialogues of Birth, Race and Memory.* Cambridge, MA, London, England: Harvard University Press, 1998.

Smith, Claudine Curry and Mildred HB Roberson. *My Bag Was Always Packed: The Life and Times of a Virginia Midwife.* Bloomington, IN, 2003. [No publisher listed.]

Smith, Margaret Charles and Linda Janet Holmes. *Listen to Me Good: The Life Story of an Alabama Midwife.* Columbus, OH: Ohio State University Press, 1996.

ARTICLES

Dawley, Katy. "Origins of Nurse-Midwifery in the United States and Its Expansion in the 1940s." *Journal of Midwifery and Women's Health.* Vol. 48, No. 2. March/April 2003.

Litoff, Judy Barrett. "The Midwife Throughout History." *Journal of Nurse-Midwifery.* Vol. 27, No. 6. November/December 1982.

Robinson, Sharon A. "A Historical Development of Midwifery in the Black Community: 1600-1940." *Journal of Nurse-Midwifery.* Vol. 29, No. 4. July/August 1984.